CATS ARE
FROM VENUS
DOGS ARE
FROM MARS

A GODSFIELD BOOK

ABOUT THE AUTHOR

Gerry Maguire Thompson's
recent humorous titles include:

Feng Shui for Dogs
The Weekend Shaman, and other New Age types
Astral Sex to Zen Teabags

In past lives, Gerry has been both a cat
and a dog - sometimes at the same time.

'All is fair in love and war'
- Anonymous

Comments on Thompson's previous work:

'Loved it – very funny, and timely'
- **Sue Townsend**, author of the Adrian Mole books

'Great swing and relish'
- **Seamus Heaney**, Nobel prizewinner for poetry

'Witty and informative'
- **Time Out** magazine, London

'Delightful and refreshing'
- **Denise Linn**, international New Age author
and workshop leader

First published in Great Britain in 1999
by Godsfield Press Ltd
A Division of David and Charles Ltd
Laurel House, Station Approach
New Alresford, Hants SO24 9JH, UK

1 3 5 7 9 10 8 6 4 2

© 1999 Godsfield Press

Text © 1999 Gerry Thompson

Designed for Godsfield Press by
The Bridgewater Book Company

Illustrations by Madeleine Hardie

Printed and bound in Italy

ISBN 1-84181-001-0

CONTENTS

The extensive research that I carried out prior to writing this book showed that there is a crying need for authoritative guidance for cats and dogs on relationship issues. All over the world, these animals are experiencing the same archetypal problems and each time 'reinventing the wheel'. This book is here, at last, to meet their heartfelt needs.

Actually, relationships were always meant to be challenging. We evolved relationship as a method of highlighting personal shortcomings, annoying habits and unresolved issues. Intimate relationship is the perfect device for two individuals to press each other's buttons. And viewed in these terms, what partnership works more effectively than that between cat and dog?

I've been travelling round the world now for fifty-nine years, giving seminars and counselling animals, my work based on the revolutionary principles contained in this marvellous book. Everywhere I go, I'm constantly moved by the heart-warming stories I hear about how

well the material works in practice. 'We just can't thank you enough,' said Tiddles and Spot, a couple from Boysey, Idaho. 'We owe everything to you.' Tiddles and Spot have now become franchised facilitators of my Partnership in Ecstasy Training™, and have become immensely rich in the process. The P.E.T. programme is now available as far afield as Outer Mongolia and Central Antarctic.

So whether you're just dating as cat-friend and dog-friend, or whether you've been living together for years, this is the book for you.

7

INTRODUCTION

It's a little-known fact that cats and dogs originated in quite different parts of our solar system and thus are totally alien species to one another. Arriving on Earth and being adopted by humans in the far distant past, they have forgotten this fundamental aspect of their history. That, essentially, is why modern cats and dogs have such disastrous relationships.

In this incredible, ground-breaking book, I directly challenge the archetypal problems and stereotyped responses of traditional cat–dog relationships. I show cats and dogs how to honour, cherish and lovingly attack one another. I offer detailed guidance on how to deepen commitment, enhance motivation, eliminate co-dependency, win fights and still get enough to eat. And I have backed all this up with material from actual relationships and real-life conversations, drawn from my vast experience in the field.

In this modern age of liberation, political correctness and enforced equality, someone has to stand out from the crowd, face up to the truth and say, 'We can't hide the truth any longer: cats and dogs *are* different.'

Using this book, cats and dogs will at last be able to really hear what each other is saying and really understand where each other is coming from. This book is very, very good. In fact, I'm completely in love with it myself.

And who knows, perhaps it could teach humans a thing or two as well.

CATS AND DOGS – ARE THEY REALLY SO DIFFERENT?

Yes, I can say categorically, they are. My years of ground-breaking research and specialized experience in this field have unequivocally convinced me that cats (species *Felis cattus*) and dogs (*Canis doggus*) have very different basic characteristics. Furthermore, I can say with authority that these different qualities profoundly influence their patterns of inter-relationship.

Cats and dogs communicate in different languages. Not only that, they want totally different things from relationships. They enjoy intimacy in contrasting ways, their goals and objectives in life are quite separate and

they experience emotions differently. Their ways of dealing with problems are also worlds apart. They're both obsessed with food, but in radically different ways. The practical effects of these differences will unfold as we progress through the book, but it may be useful to introduce some of the key elements here.

★ Dogs and cats have different ways of coping with stress. Cats deal with stress by falling asleep. Dogs deal with it by forgetting what it was that was causing them stress.

★ Cats and dogs are motivated by different things. Dogs are motivated by loyalty, competitiveness, the quest for food, the sight of a dog lead, the quest for food, *joie-de-vivre*, the throwing of sticks and the quest for food. Cats aren't really motivated about anything.

★ Cat and dog fixations on food are different. Dog interest in food focuses mainly on how much of it there is, while cat emphasis is mainly to do with how expensive it was to buy.

★ Dogs have a conscience, look guilty and give the game away. Dogs have to tell the truth. Cats are untroubled by such shortcomings.

★ Cats spend many hours pondering on the nature of existence. Dogs are not really deep thinkers. A typical dog train of thought lasts about seven milliseconds.

★ Dogs are creatures of action, excitement, adventure and exercise. They love cars, sport, racing, going out drinking, pottering around and DIY. Cats just can't see the point of any of this.

In order to improve their relationship with one another, cats and dogs need to understand what makes each other tick, rather than write each other off merely as pointless, defective aliens. They need to be able to think like one another.

So a cat needs to be able to think like a dog. She needs to remember, for instance, that dogs have no inherent sense of right and wrong. They are simple creatures, who only understand simple commands, clear gestures, firm treatment and painful punishment. And the dog needs to be able to think like a cat. He must try to remember that cats do not mentally focus on usefulness and purpose, that it is enough for a cat to just 'be' – a concept that is difficult for him to even begin to grasp.

If cats and dogs can begin to understand why each other feels the way it does, then they'll be able to communicate better, celebrate their differences, negotiate more effectively, inflict more pain upon one another and generally enjoy a far more fulfilling relationship.

HOW CATS AND DOGS TALK
TO EACH OTHER

Because they're alien species, the methods of communication that cats and dogs use are different. A typical cat–dog conversation might start something like this:

She: 'Why don't you ever listen to me?'

He: 'What's that, darling?'

Cats like to gossip about things that dogs may consider trivial minutiae, but which to cats are basic life issues. Things like shopping, how much food costs, which fish is currently seasonal and how un-busy they've been today. Dogs like talking about sticks, football, how far they've run, their latest sexual conquests, how much territory they've got and the colour of their poo. But that's only when dogs do talk.

For the most part, they'd far rather be out doing things. When dogs talk, they are straightforward and literal. They are hopeless at hidden agendas, subtle innuendo or barbed ironic remarks. Cats, however, have mastery of subtle and indirect communication, and creative exaggeration. Cats can also use pointed silences very effectively, though these are a bit wasted on dogs.

Listening skills are crucial to relationships, and here too cats and dogs have differing abilities. Cats listen to what's being said only when they are being stroked, cuddled or otherwise appreciated. Dogs only listen when

their name is spoken. What they hear is a series of blurred mumblings, interspersed with occasional clear mentions of their name. Take Tiddles and Spot, for instance – a couple who came to me for counselling because they were experiencing communication difficulties. I told Tiddles that if she wants Spot to concentrate on what she is saying, she should insert his name into every sentence. For instance, she could say something like this:

'Spot! Are you listening to me, Spot? Good, Spot. Now, Spot, I'm going to say something very important. (Insert important message here), Spot. Okay, Spot?'

Better still, she could find ways of cunningly working his name into her message, while referring to something else. For instance, she could say:

★ 'Get me a *spot* of milk, would you?' Or:

★ 'I've just *spotted* a dog who's much better-looking than you.' Or indeed:

★ 'I've got a *spot* on my nose. Would you squeeze it for me?'

And now for the dogs. Instead of listening skills, you have to develop other techniques that will make up. A useful ploy is to appear to be listening very carefully to what your cat-friend is saying, when you've completely blanked out. Fix your gaze steadily on her, holding your ears upright and pointing them toward her. That way she will really feel heard.

DO YOU HEAR WHAT I'M SAYING?

Cats and dogs used to be able to understand each other, but now they have forgotten how to do it. The trouble is, when a cat says something to a dog, he hears something quite different from what she meant. He interprets what she has said in terms of what it would mean to his own people. And when the dog speaks to the cat, she hears whatever that would mean to her race which is something completely different from what the dog was meaning to say.

Take Butch and Katikins, for instance – another couple who were having communication problems. By the time I saw them, things had already deteriorated to a state of near-crisis.

Conversations between Katikins and Butch would go something like this. Butch would come home after a hard day of running round the neighbourhood with his mates, foraging in trash cans and barking at strangers, to find Katikins in an agitated state, and say:

'Woof, woof.'

When Butch says this, what Katikins hears is this:

'Oh, Katikins, I can see you're really under pressure. Is there anything I can do to help?'

But what Butch really meant was: 'Woof, woof.'

So Katikins answers:

'Miaow, miaow.'

Meaning: 'You're a worthless piece of trash and you don't really care how I am. You're not interested in me in the slightest. All my problems are your fault.' Katikins now

wants to hear Butch say: 'Oh dear, you poor thing. Please complain to me about it for several hours.' But Butch heard: 'Miaow, miaow,' meaning: 'Miaow, miaow.' And he replies: 'Where's my dinner?'

These discrepancies stem from the opposite ways that cats and dogs deal with life. Cats expect others to be intuitively aware of their needs. Dogs just ask for what they want. This is why Butch and Katikins were having problems understanding one another. After intensive counselling, they began to make progress with their relationship and their communication. Butch began to understand that when Katikins said 'Miaow,' she meant, 'You're a waste of skin.'

This kind of communication is clearly less than ideal; these two obviously want quite different things. Katikins wants to feel loved, supported and cherished, and to be horrible to Butch. Butch's needs are simpler: he wants his dinner. Katikins needs to realize that it is sometimes hard for Butch to give her his whole attention when he hasn't eaten yet. And Butch needs to realize that no matter how much Katikins really feels heard, she isn't going to stop complaining. In fact, nothing he can do is ever going to be enough. In the end, Butch found peace of mind when he stopped worrying about it and focused instead on getting dinner and falling asleep. Unfortunately, Katikins went off her food, and died.

THE DOG AND CAT PHRASE BOOK

Cat phrases, and what they mean in Dog Language:

'I love you' = *'Get me some cream'*

'I love you very much' = *'Get me some cream now'*

'I'll never love anyone else' = *'I'll kill you*
if you don't get me some cream right now'

'HHHHSSSSSSSS!' = *'Leave me alone'*

'Leave me alone' = *'Pay me some attention'*

'Help!' = *Dog language has no equivalent for this expression,*
because dogs don't ask for help.

Dog phrases, and what they mean in Cat Language:

'I love you' = *'I love you'*

'I love you very much' = *'I love you very much'*

'I'll never love anyone else' = *'I'll never love anyone else'*

'Leave me alone' = *'Leave me alone' etc., etc., etc.*

THINGS NEVER TO SAY

Here are some things a dog
should never say to a cat:

'I don't care.'

'It's all your fault.'

'You're wrong.'

'You wouldn't understand.'

**And here are some things a cat
should never say to a dog:**

Nothing. Cats can say whatever they want to dogs.

DEALING WITH PROBLEMS

Cats and dogs are worlds apart in how they react to problems in a relationship.

When a cat is overwhelmed and under pressure, she wants to let everyone know that she is suffering. She likes to get together with some friends in the middle of the night and wail about it. But when a dog doesn't know how to cope with things, his response is quite different. He needs to get his head together; he needs to get away from the cat; he needs to go to his kennel.

Snoopy and Loopy are two individuals who find this coming up a lot. When Snoopy comes home after a stressful day at work, his way of feeling better is to relax. But Loopy's way of feeling better is to yell and scream at Snoopy. So tension quickly builds up. Loopy can soon feel ignored, while Snoopy feels harassed.

In this situation, Loopy would keep pushing Snoopy further in an attempt to draw him out, and eventually bite a piece out of his ear. Snoopy would immediately lash out at Loopy, who was invariably quick enough to evade his blow. A breakneck chase round the room would follow, complete with broken ornaments and shredded upholstery. Loopy would be too quick and nimble for Snoopy, who would go into a huff and declare that he was going to his kennel. When Snoopy retreats to his kennel, it is very easy for Loopy to think: 'This is terrible. It's the end of the world. Who am I going to torment now? I feel awful. I need some cream.'

25

I explained to Loopy that time spent in the kennel is a very important part of any dog's life. In the kennel, he can get his mind back to the most important concern in life: how to get more food. What Snoopy is really saying is: 'I think I'll just lie down for a bit. When I get up, I'll be hungry again, and hunger always wipes my mind clear of whatever was in it before.' This is a dog's way of dealing with problems. For Loopy, however, it's understandable to worry at this point: when a dog stops trying to tear a cat to pieces, she will naturally tend to take it personally. She wants him to come out so she can make his life hell.

I told Loopy that the best thing she can do is to have a good time by herself. When Snoopy realizes that Loopy is enjoying herself, he'll soon be ready to get back to the good old rough-and-tumble, spit and flying fur.

Things a cat can do when the dog is upset and in his kennel:

★ Go out fishing
★ Get a professional grooming
★ Eat the dog's food
★ See a therapist
★ Go shopping
★ Nothing

UNDERSTANDING YOUR PARTNER'S EMOTIONS

In order to relate properly, it is essential for cats and dogs to understand each other's very different emotional patterns. This can be a challenging process, but if I explain one or two of these patterns and what they mean it will help you understand your partner a whole lot better.

Generally speaking, it is much easier for the cat to understand the dog's emotional patterns than the other way round. This is because dogs don't really have many emotional patterns. Basically, dogs are always feeling either ecstatic enthusiasm or excruciating boredom, and that's about it. Of course, they also experience deep lusts for food, sex and exercise, but in emotional terms these all manifest as irrepressible enthusiasm. Boredom is what happens when they've just finished being irrepressibly enthusiastic and are waiting for the next bit of irrepressible enthusiasm to come along.

Cats, on the other hand, are a lot more emotionally complex. Some of the commonest emotions that they display include envy, greed, jealousy, hatred, spitefulness, aloofness and weirdness. In fact, they experience the whole gamut of emotions that are displayed by humans, plus a few extra that cats have made up for themselves. I have discovered that this major difference is due to the fact that dogs lack the X chromosome possessed by cats.

This lack also explains why dogs have less sensitivity, subtlety and capacity for social adjustment.

In their interactions, cats and dogs need to take these differences into account. Otherwise it is very easy for the cat to embrace the stereotyped image of the dog as an unfeeling lump with all the subtlety of a bull in a china shop. Likewise, there is an overriding tendency for the dog to see the cat as an unpredictable and capricious drama queen who is always making a fuss over nothing. Each needs to appreciate what is really going on for the other and so step out of the traditional patterns of response. A dog, then, needs to find ways of showing that he understands what a cat is feeling, when he doesn't and never will. The cat, correspondingly, needs to

discover ways of showing that she even cares what the dog is feeling, which is actually an even more remote possibility.

Cats and dogs both have distinctive ways of expressing affection and commitment in relationship, and it is important for each of them to be able to recognize these indicators of appreciation and cherish them. The dog's favourite way of expressing appreciation for the cat is by falling asleep while she is talking to him. And the cat's most emphatic expression of acceptance of the dog is through attempting to scratch his eyes out. This is the feline equivalent of the human emotional phenomenon known as Pre Menstrual Syndrome, except that it happens all the time. So remember, dogs, that this kind of gesture is only the cat's way of strengthening the bond between the two of you.

WHAT ABOUT MY NEEDS?

Cats and dogs have differing emotional needs, which very much affect the way they inter-relate. Cats want reassurance; they need to hear something said repetitively and consistently if they are to feel assured that it is true, otherwise they quickly stop believing it. But dogs tend to say something once, and then presume that it will be taken as true until they say something different. This is an issue for another couple who came to me for help, Beefy and Fifi.

Here's how a typical conversation between them would go.

Fifi: 'Do you love me?'

Beefy: 'Of course I love you.'

Fifi: 'Why don't you ever tell me you love me?'

Beefy: 'I did tell you I love you.'

Fifi: 'But that was a year ago.'

Beefy: 'Well, it's still true. OK?'

There is clearly a difference of perspective here. At this point, Beefy thinks the matter has been cleared up, but Fifi feels unheard and uncared for. As the conversation continues, the difference in communication patterns becomes even more clear:

Fifi: 'Well, how am I to know that you still love me when you don't tell me?'

Beefy: 'Have I told you that I don't love you any more?'

Fifi: 'No.'

Beefy: 'Did I say, "By the way, I hate you"?'

Fifi: 'No …'

Beefy: 'Well, that means I still love you. OK?'

This isn't the kind of reassurance that Fifi is looking for; furthermore, Beefy is now beginning to feel as if a big fuss is being made about nothing. I told Beefy and Fifi that they would have to become aware of this difference if they were going to improve their communication and strengthen their relationship.

Dogs also need to feel that they're terribly important and like to be reassured of this importance. So when the dog does feel like talking, the cat should always pretend that she's interested in what the dog has to say, even though she never is. She should make sympathetic and interested noises, such as 'Mmm, I see,' or 'Oh really?' No matter how dull he is and how deficient his conversation skills, she should act as if he is absolutely fascinating and riveting to listen to. She won't have to be very good at acting – the dog will be naturally inclined to believe it anyway. She might want to steer him away, though, from dog subjects that are especially boring or about which he is inclined to go on interminably – e.g. sticks, football and himself.

Furthermore, dogs need reassuring that they are incredibly strong, powerful and frightening, that they are always in control and that they generally make the world work properly. When they feel assured of this by cats, they then sit back and do nothing, so cats can get on with the job of really getting affairs into order – mainly by falling asleep.

INTIMACY

Intimacy is a key component of close relationships; any partnership that neglects it will soon be in trouble. Cats and dogs, however, have different ideas of how much intimacy is enough.

For instance, Fuzzywuzzy was in a promising relationship with Gnasher. They appeared to be moving steadily toward a deeper level of commitment, though were not yet living together. One day, Fuzzywuzzy called Gnasher on the phone and said she felt they needed to spend some 'quality time' together: to share some intimate moments, chill out, have a nice time and just see what happens. So Gnasher agreed, and invited Fuzzywuzzy round for a pleasant and intimate evening.

When Fuzzywuzzy arrives, however, she finds that Gnasher's friends Rover, Rufus, Fido and Rex are also there. What Gnasher has arranged is that they all spend the evening together – watching TV, fighting, drinking beer and establishing a canine hierarchy of authority. This is not, of course, what Fuzzywuzzy had in mind. As Fuzzywuzzy leaves at the end of the evening, Gnasher tells her how much he enjoyed it and how glad he is that they had been able to really get close. Next day, Gnasher is genuinely bewildered when Fuzzywuzzy calls the whole thing off.

Another case springs to mind here. Bubbles and Shep are a couple who live together. They both lead busy, professional lives, each doing their own thing for most of their time. Shep has a hectic schedule of ransacking garbage cans, burying bones, patrolling his territory and following his master round the house every time he gets up from his chair. Bubbles, meanwhile, packs her days with refusing her food, looking out through the window and sleeping a great deal.

All this limits the amount of time they can spend together. But they each assess that all-important 'intimacy quotient' differently. This shows in the way they report to their respective friends at the weekend.

'Yes, it's been a good week for me and Bubbles,' says Shep to his mates, as they scrounge potato chips from the humans in the local bar. 'We really saw a lot of each other. We got to spend three evenings together.'

This is greeted by compli-
mentary remarks like,
'Exemplary commitment,
man!' and, 'You're far too
good to that cat.'
Meanwhile, Bubbles is
shooting the breeze with
her cronies in the back-
yard, catching up on local

gossip and complaining about the deterioration of the
neighbourhood. 'It's been a terrible week for Shep and
me,' she grumbles. 'We've hardly seen anything of one
another. We only spent three evenings together.' This is
greeted by a chorus of 'Disgraceful' and 'Ditch the
bastard!' Same week; different point of view.

Ultimately, this scenario can threaten the whole
relationship. Shep becomes increasingly complacent,
thinking that things are going incredibly well, while
Bubbles is experiencing it as a living nightmare, a
relationship in its last death-throes. Which it soon is.
Same relationship; different point of view.

The fact is that cats thrive on intimacy. It is the drug they crave; and no matter how much there is, it is never enough. Most dogs, though, shy away from intimacy. They find it pointless at best, embarrassing at worse. To them, it lacks practical purpose. Indeed, any kind of declaration of affection is anathema to a dog – unless of course it involves a human being, which for some reason they have no problem with.

As we have already discovered, dogs just do not enjoy saying to a cat, 'I love you.' There are a million reasons not to say it. They think it's too sissy. It's not 'cool'. They've already said it before. They're too busy. And so on, and so on.

What every dog–cat couple needs to do to resolve this dilemma is to find acceptable ways of saying 'I love you' – forms of uttering those magic words that the cat can use without unduly nauseating the dog, and that the dog can say to the cat without blowing his reputation as a tough dude. Here are some examples.

Acceptable coded dog ways of saying 'I love you' to a cat:

'Hi.'

'Nice day, isn't it?'

'You're looking good today.'

'I hate you.'

Acceptable disguised cat ways of saying 'I love you' to a dog:

'Hi, big boy.'

'Can I feel your muscles?'

'Eat claw, shit-face.'

'I hate you too.'

NASTY AND ANNOYING HABITS

Annoying habits are an important aspect of any cat–dog partnership. Indeed, each partner tends to think of the other primarily as a bundle of habits ranging from the irritating to the infuriating. It's most important that each party recognizes its own aggravating ways and takes responsibility for them, thus maximising their detrimental effects on the opposition. The key element in all this is understanding how one's habits are perceived by the other side.

Cats see dogs essentially as a package of disgusting and nauseating traits. Dogs never wash themselves properly. They think that grooming is a waste of time. They greet one another by sniffing each other's rear end. They do things in public that should really be done in private. They leave excremental offerings on display on public sidewalks. They have sex publicly in broad daylight. They lick their genitals with abandon, no matter who's watching. They even try to have sex with the legs of human beings. They eat the most appalling and revolting things.

Furthermore, dogs bark persistently for no apparent reason. They chew your mail as soon as it drops through the letterbox. They're desperate to please. They look at you with mournful, pleading eyes when they want something. They hate keeping still, even for thirty seconds; they need constant stimulation. They're possessive: they want you to be their friend and no-one else's. They're paranoid about formal male structuring among themselves: they need to know exactly where they stand in relation to everyone else in the hierarchy.

Dogs see cats' habits as characterized by neurotic self-obsession, narcissism, indolence and anal retentiveness. Cats rarely do anything constructive or useful, yet they always seem to get fed. They never fetch a newspaper or bark at strangers. If a burglar breaks into the home in the middle of the night, the cat will be happy as long as she gets given some milk. They sit right in front of the fire so no-one else can get any heat and they can't tolerate the slightest draught. They preen and groom and pamper themselves incessantly. They can spend an hour washing even if they were spotless when they started. They're extremely fussy about what they eat, what company they keep and a thousand other things. They select a spot to sit with fanatical care and many changes of mind. They just seem to love themselves to death. Oh yes, and they never stop yawning.

Cats are incredibly sneaky about everything they do. They're ultra discreet about where they leave their droppings, which dogs can't even begin to understand; after all, what's the point of producing the stuff if you don't use it for self-advertising? Cats may pursue their sexual proclivities in the middle of the night when there's no-one around, but they make a hell of a racket in the process. And cats can be disgusting in their own way: no dog can beat a cat for creating a stinky litter tray. Cats love to catch hapless little birds or mice, bite their heads off and leave their mutilated remains on display to impress humans; more bizarrely still, they don't even eat the corpses. Cats display a streak of cruelty that dogs can never get near. Like those little birds and mice, for instance – you can be sure that before they were finally finished off, they spent their last hours in long-drawn-out torture, having first been handicapped by the removal of a limb or two; cats think of this as some sort of grotesque 'game'. Cats are fond of sneaking round soundlessly and then springing on you from nowhere to give you the fright of your life.

All in all, then, cats and dogs have a lot to cope with if they are going to accept each other's annoying habits. My advice to them is not to bother. Because let's face it – some things will never change.

CONFLICT

The issue of conflict is a central concern in any relationship, and never more so than with cats and dogs. Conflict can do a great deal of damage, and leave one or both partners scarred for life – not only psychologically, but physically too.

What my research has shown is that conflict is not a bad thing. In fact, it can be very creative, and should not be avoided or suppressed. I explain to my clients that any partnership that consists purely of lovey-dovey cuddliness, sweetness and light is a complete sham.

Underneath the surface, it is a seething hotbed of emotional denial, suppressed rage, bitterness and hatred – a volcano ready to explode at any moment. Far better, I tell them, to let out all the bitterness, hatred and rage. As cats and dogs, you already know this in your heart of hearts. So don't feel guilty about it. Connect with that hidden tiger lurking just under the surface, or the savage wolf beneath the thin veneer of civilisation. Just enjoy it.

The object in any cat-and-dog partnership, then, is to maximize the creative potential that conflict holds – so really go to town, and squeeze every last bit of value from it. Keep conflict alive, and your relationship will always have a solid basis in deep and lasting enmity.

SHAMING AND BLAMING

Apportioning blame is one of the commonest sources of conflict in relationship. Humans reckon it is important to listen without blaming, but cats and dogs must learn instead to blame without listening. Both need to work at cultivating this ability, because each finds it difficult. Dogs are good at not listening, but not very good at blaming – it's far too complex and analytical for them.

They're much more interested in what's going to happen next, than in who's to blame for what already happened. Cats, on the other hand, are very good at blaming, but hopeless at not listening. This is because their legendary curiosity always gets the better of them – part of their mind is always thinking that there might be something juicy coming up in whatever anyone is saying. This is why cats listen even when they're fast asleep.

Nevertheless, blame can still be used creatively as a source of conflict. Cats can be particularly adept at escaping blame when they're guilty. With those great big innocent eyes, they seem to say, 'What, me? I wouldn't do anything like that.' To make matters worse, cats are incredibly intuitive and can tell immediately when they're being deceived, while dogs are totally useless at lying. Even humans can tell when dogs are lying.

GETTING YOUR OWN WAY

In the early days of relationship counselling, both partners were urged to engage in yielding and self-sacrifice to avoid 'rocking the boat'. Today, I tell my clients, giving in is a no-no. Compromise is out. Low self-esteem is a personal crime. Self-assertiveness is the buzzword these days.

You owe it to the wellbeing of your relationship to dominate your partner completely. You can't have a top cat and top dog living in the same household; after all, you're not human beings. The real trick, though, is to get your partner to do exactly what you want without appearing to be controlling. This calls for subtlety and deviousness (so dogs are going to be at a disadvantage here).

In fact, cats are always going to do a better job of manipulative domination. However, you need to exercise care. Take the partnership of Fluffy and Scruffy, for instance – a classic example of how you can take controlling your partner too far. When Fluffy met Scruffy, she was immediately attracted, though she could see he was a real mess. Scruffy was lethargic and overweight. He never got his hair cut. His nose was dry and he had awful dog-breath. He couldn't even hold down a job bringing the daily paper home. And he was addicted to television. Scruffy was a real down-and-out. Yet Fluffy thought to herself: 'I can save this dog. Through being with me, he is going to become a success story and we shall live happily ever after!'

But that's not what happened. Instead, Scruffy got worse; soon he could not even be bothered watching day-time TV. And the more Fluffy tried to improve him, the worse he got. So she came to me for counselling. After a number of sessions, she was able to see that this was a repeating pattern. She had always been attracted to derelict dogs who have nothing going for them. She would always try to change them into her idea of what a dog should be; and she would always fail and then blame herself.

Eventually, she saw that it was all to do with her family background. Her own father had been a disreputable individual who only came by when Fluffy's mother was in season and then disappeared again. Fluffy had never even met him. Now she was spending her life seeking out losers and trying to transform them. This was clearly not going to succeed. Through deep work on her personal issues, though, Fluffy eventually managed to reverse this tendency. Now she's a far happier cat. She's stopped trying to change Scruffy. He's still a complete slob, but she doesn't mind, because she's become a complete slob too.

Nevertheless, even though you won't be able to alter your partner's persona, there are still important aspects in which you can get your own way. So remember:

★ Encourage and reinforce acceptable behaviour by being sweet and nice.

★ Discourage unacceptable behaviour by punishment and ruthless cruelty.

SPEAKING BODY LANGUAGE

Cats and dogs, of course, have completely different body language. Understanding what your partner is really saying to you through his or her physical behaviour will assist you greatly in deepening the relationship and generally getting your own way. The important distinction you need to be able to make is between when your partner should be taken seriously – sometimes a matter of life and death – and when he or she is merely 'trying it on', which is most of the time. Here are some important examples of body language, together with what they mean for you in practice.

CAT BODY LANGUAGE FOR DOGS

★ Rubbing up against you: she wants something – this is a favourable time to negotiate.

★ Standing her ground, arching her back, hissing, sticking her fur out and generally looking like a bristle brush:

don't push your luck, buddy.

★ Running round the house like a mad thing, careering all over the curtains: you're driving her up the walls – keep doing whatever you're doing.

★ Scratching your eyes out: can be a sign either of disapproval or of acceptance.

DOG BODY LANGUAGE FOR CATS

★ Looking as tall as possible, hairs standing up on neck, lip curling, snarling a lot: whatever you want can wait.

★ Keeping low, tail tucked under, ears flat against head: abject fear – a good time for you to attack.

★ Rolling on back, exposing tummy: submission – carte blanche for you.

★ Tail wagging: doesn't mean anything – basically, it's an indication that the dog is still alive.

NEW AGE PARTNERS

The different facets of the so-called New Age have brought yet more concerns to inter-species relationships.

First there was feminism and political correctness and a whole new set of rules to abide by in addition to the already formidable array. Roles were re-defined and new protocols established. It seemed you could never do anything right, especially if you were a dog.

Still, there were certain advantages for the canine species. For instance, the cat might once have scampered up a tree, got stuck there and then expected you to run off like in some movie, find a fire-fighter, tug at their sleeve and psychically tell them that she's in trouble and that they have to come and save her. Now, though, you could say, 'No – you're always wanting to be so independent and post-feminist – you can just get yourself down from the tree. Anyways, I'm far too busy burying this bone.'

Then there was the 'New Dog' syndrome. Dogs suddenly thought they had to be working on their 'feminine aspect', pretending they were some kind of cat – refusing food, purring, offering to do the washing-up, that kind of thing. It was a complete disaster. Dogs

were totally hopeless at it and cats thought they were pathetic. Cats don't want a New Dog, they want a Real Dog – virile, aggressive, straightforward, insensitive, nothing like a cat. They want something to pit their wits against, something to get their teeth into.

Thankfully all this has gone now. And some of the recent New Age archetypes seem somewhat more attractive. The fashionable New Age cat mode is Zen meditation and she can really get into that. So ninety-

eight percent of her time she can spend 'just being'; then she can suddenly spring into an explosive burst of samurai furball, the mistress of the oriental martial arts who can kill at a stroke. It's a pretty good combination.

The trend-setting New Age dog is exploring the Way of the Warrior and he loves it. He can relish his Neanderthal identity, savouring the role of the primitive hunter-gatherer. But he can also acknowledge his Inner Wimp, when it suits him, and still get away with it – like when the opposition is just too scary. So he's got a great option too.

One word of caution, though – you can carry this New Age thing too far. Tantric sex between cats and dogs is just not a good idea.

ONE LAST WORD

These differences between cats and dogs run very deep; it usually takes around twenty years to understand and overcome them. Since few of you live beyond the age of fifteen, however, this presents quite a challenge. Perhaps that's why things never seem to change much between cats and dogs.

Oh well, at least you don't tell each other what to wear.

ACKNOWLEDGEMENTS

I thank my dog Vergil for showing me my own insight, powerfulness, beauty, skill, genius, greatness and sheer humility.

I recognize my cat Scrumpkins for simply being.

I cherish Elaine Bellamy, Rhoda Nottridge and Hazel Weldon for inspiration, support and Chinese take-out food.

My heartfelt gratitude goes out to all at Godsfield Press and Bridgewater Books, those literary midwives who strove night and day to help birth this project.

And I honour most of all myself, without whom none of it would have been possible.

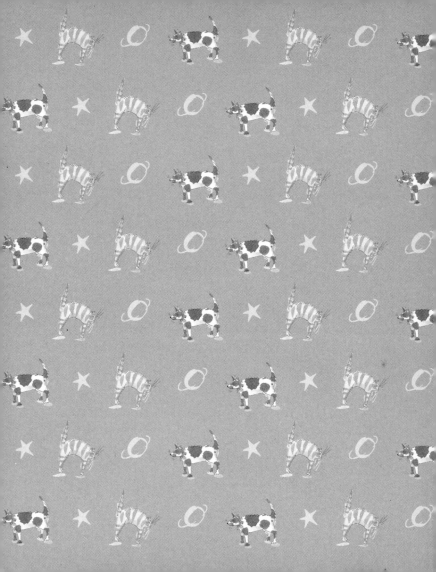